My Town

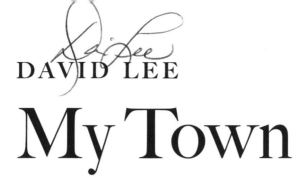

DAVID LEE

My Town

COPPER CANYON PRESS

Copyright © 1995 by David Lee.

Publication of this book is supported by a grant from the National
Endowment for the Arts and a grant from the Lannan Foundation.
Additional support to Copper Canyon Press has been provided by the
Andrew W. Mellon Foundation, the Lila Wallace–Reader's Digest
Fund, and the Washington State Arts Commission. Copper Canyon
Press is in residence with Centrum at Fort Worden State Park.

The Western States Book Awards are a project of the Western States
Arts Federation. The awards are supported by Crane Duplicating
Services, the Elaine Horwitch Memorial Culture Fund (Arnold
Horwitch, Trustee), and the Witter Bynner Foundation for Poetry.
Additional funding is provided by the National Endowment for
the Arts.

Library of Congress Cataloging-in-Publication Data

Lee, David, 1944 Aug. 13–
My town / David Lee
p. cm.
ISBN 1-55659-074-1
1. City and town life – Utah – Poetry. 1. Title
PS3562.E338M9 1995
811'.54 – DC20   95-17053

0 9 8 7 6 5 4 3 2

COPPER CANYON PRESS
P.O. BOX 271, PORT TOWNSEND, WASHINGTON 98368

Grateful acknowledgment is made to the editors of the following magazines in which these poems first appeared:

American Literary Review
City Art
Cutbank
Ellipsis
Hayden's Ferry Review
Hurākan
Jeopardy
Kenyon Review
Nebraska Territory
Neon
Ploughshares
Poetry East
Puerto del Sol
River Styx
Story
Tailwind
Tumblewords Anthology
Utah English Journal
Weber Studies
Willow Springs

AUTHOR'S ACKNOWLEDGMENTS: the author wishes to thank Southern Utah University for a sabbatical leave during which this book took its final shape. Special thanks to Mistah David Clewell, Katie Coles and Bill Holm for criticism and advice above and beyond the call of friendship; to the Nebraska connection: Brummels, Lar, Gilbert, Kloefkorn, et al.; to Mark and Susan: happy trails, bless you; to Ken Brewer, adopted brother; to Jeanne Clark; to Jan, Jon and Jodee for standing by me. "Faith Tittle" is for Kay Cook and Julie Simon. "Haystacking" is for Dan and Sybil Cockrum. "Idyll" is for Leslie and Kitty Norris.

For My Parents
Chant and Ruth Lee
With Love

&

For Bill and Eloise Kloefkorn
Likewise, With Love

CONTENTS

3 Prelude

4 Terrace Mound

6 Ugly

12 Fruit Trees

14 Preacher

19 Deaf

21 Doc

28 Bryant Willliamson

33 Clean

35 Barbed Wire

39 Faith Tittle

44 Fast

47 Potts Coal Mine, Inc.

53 Lazy

57 The Sawmill Road

64 No Lazy S. Ranch

73 Interlude

76 Curley

80 Jesse

82 Vera

86 Broken Leg

90 The Wart

105 Idyll

106 Haystacking

114 Brothers

116 The Landrum Geese

126 Bobby Joe

127 Willie and the Water Pipe

132 Postlude

135 Benediction

My Town

Prelude

You can't go home again
T. WOLFE

That's shit
BILL HOLM

Who sed that?
Did somebody say that
or was it in one of them dam books you read?

It don't matter
it's a pile of crap
I go home ever day
don't matter where I am
I'm the prodigal son coming back
I don't even need a Greyhound bus
I can go to my town right now
right here talking to you
because this
is everywhere
I've ever been

Terrace Mound

Go through them gates
and turn left

them's the Rushings
had the little grocery store
after he quit farming
and there's Maloufs
they's immigrants
spoze most of us are
they took a later boat
had this boy Tommy
with the cancer in high school
that played football
chopped him off a part at a time
had a thumb and a little finger
on that one hand
then they took his thumb
and a leg
he give it up

Kay Stokes down there
with the big fence
and the Patricks next door
them's the expensive people
Bryant Williams down a little further
turn there

here's Edna Mae Garner and Rufus
way down there at the end
with the white picket fence is Lela's
and over there in that flat place

in the sun is Ellis Britton
should of planted a tree there
be shade for the whole block
my Lard I couldn't of told you
what Buck Gosset's name was
2 minutes ago if I hadn't seen it

down to the left
at the end of that street's
a Gypsy come in with the carnival
got in a knife fight
over one of the wormen
so he stayed

and acrost that street
right down there, see?
was a man I loved
that's Mr. Cummings's place
and up from him

Ugly

Ugliest man in town
was Raphael Martinez
he's kin to them Martinezes
I never told you about
had them triplet boys
2 borned hooked together on one leg
and this sister
that grown a extra tit
right above her hip they sed
but they never cut them apart
borned dead
so they took the 2
and put them in a museum
in a jar where you
can go see them
looking at you through the alcohol
he wasn't born that way

herded sheep up above sawmill road
this one morning he woke up
wished he hadn't of
couldn't stand up the pain was so bad
he known he couldn't live with it
and it was too far to town
like a weasel inside him
chewing he said
he found his pistol
put it in his mouth and pulled
bullet torn out his cheekbone
shot off half his ear

never hit no brains at all
and that was the only bullet left
he couldn't get to the rifle

so after he waited to die
and finally didn't
taken his knife
cut his throat but didn't hit a vein
stabbed hisself but the blade
was turned wrong
on a rib and bounced off
stabbed hisself higher
and harder
hit his collarbone so it broke
the knifeblade off
part of it stuck in the bone
he thrown hisself in the fire

sed that hurt too bad to stay
it was coals from last night
melted his face on one part
burnt off the hair on that side
where it never did grown back
closed up one eye
carterized his neck
where he cut it so it almost stopped bleeding
sed he could hear hisself frying
for somebody's breakfast
but he had to roll out
couldn't stand it no more
found a shoeing hammer
took and hit hisself
hard as he could
between the eyes
with both hands on the handle

knocked him out so hard
he should of starved to death
before he woke up
but didn't
had a lump the size
of a ostrich egg growing on his face
so he had one more idea

tied a pigging rope on his feet
drug hisself to this mule he had
a mean kicking bastard
crawlt up on his back
and tied his hands to his feet
under that mule's belly
sed he never known how that mule
let him get on he's hollering so
of the pain when he moved
that mule hated being loaded
and he'd even untied him first
he could of run off or kicked him
in the mouth there on his knees
he figgered that mule
would at least thrown him off
over his butt and kick loose
cave mebbe the rest of his head in
mule turnt and went to town

got him there by afternoon
passed out
people who found him was scairt to death
seen that one side
didn't have no face left
blood all over that mule
like he'd been swatting flies on him
with a icepick
they took him to the hospital

couldn't figure out what was wrong
saw all them holes in him
burnt off spots
blood everwhere
when they went
to lay him out straight he'd scream
like hell and they couldn't understand
a word of it
the only English he's speaking
was Spanish
couldn't wake him up enough
to shift his gear
tried to patch him up
best they could
without it costing much
they known it wasn't no insurance
nobody wanted the mule

that night they sed
he set up hollering like a sonofabitch
grapt his privates like
he'd pull it off
they taken and given him a shot
by next morning
he passed as big as the end of your thumb
this kidney stone
sed it turnt his gentile inside out
never seen one that big before
he bored a hole in it
worn it for a necklace
I seen it many a time
my god he's ugly

about half a face
with the eye shut on that side

half a ear
throat cut scar and his arms
blistered from his elbows to hands
where he lain in that fire
dent between his eyes
and a big white spot
where his cheekbone used to be
before the bullet come out
wasn't a kid in town
who'd stay on the same side the street
as he's walking on
never bothered him a bit
he's happy as a goose
and about that many brains left

so about a year before he died
he come in to the doctor again
all wadded up in a bunch
his kinfolk brought him
give him the examination
and the x-ray by then
doctor sez I got bad news for you
sed his face went as white
as a Nazarine preacher or a highway patrol
doctor sez you got the cancer
Ralph Martinez almost fell off the chair

started laughing and bawling
did the cross thing
sed oh thank god goddam thank god
I's afraid it'd be the kidney stone again
he's so happy they sed
it almost looked like that face
would of busted like a balloon
sed he wasn't afraid of no cancer
or dying cause he been there before

but with the kidney stone
it wasn't no way he could find out
how to not be there when it happened
and that's just too ugly
for him to have to think about

Fruit Trees

See them 4 trees out there?
They been in 8 years
haven't had one apple or pear yet
I believe that grocery store
he grafted box elder on
except that kind would of grown
them won't even do that

back home ever fall at the fair
they had a fruit judging
from whoever's trees wanted
to bring it in to be looked over
2 years in a row this Jesus Salinas
kept the graveyard mowed and watered
dug and filt graves up
planted some fruit trees in a row
won the blue ribbon
second time for peaches, apples, pears
and persimmons I think
about ever one they had

bunch of other people
pitched a hissey
sed it wasn't fair
he never owned that land
them trees was on
belonged to the county
and the dead people who paid
to be there
it wasn't one inch his
Ellis Britton never even

got a white ribbon for 5th
sez besides he's got a unfair vantage
being borned in Mexico
naturally good at it
sed it aint no way
the rest of us can get
that much fertilizer down that deep
he sez yougn either pick anothern
by god I'll go out there
and chop ever dam tree
in the graveyard down
it won't be no fruit or shade
left for nobody out there
to lean up against waiting
I don't have to put up
with this one minute
you caint take away
my taxpaying rights

judge had to start over
pick a fair winner
they'd all agree to and make sure
Ellis got some kind of ribbon
after it was over sed
when he died they ought to plant
a bannar tree on Ellis Britton's grave
enough fertilizer
to put Cuba out of business
if it didn't burn the tree up

them of mine
got one more year
if it ain't no fruit
I ain't driving very far
to get some firewood
that's a fact

Preacher

In 1956 Baptists got a new preacher
Reverent Pastor Brother Strayhan
from the Southern Tennessee preacher school seminary
he had a Bible they give him
for graduating had about 40 ribbons
marking his page number
hanging out the back
ever color you could imagine
after he'd been there about a year
still tell them about how
they didn't appreciate him enough
because he was awarded them ribbons
for being outstanding in his field
one day Mizrez Bouchier
who was old enough to not care no more
sed after church she wished
he'd go back and stand
out in his field some more
she had enuf of him arredy

he'd preach swinging that thing
round like a Chinaman's kite
by the end the sermon
he'd took out the ribbons marking spots
all worked up to give the invitation
swung it so hard oncet
them ribbons chopped the top
off a incarnation in the pulpit flowerpot

he loved to preach on how
he got calt by the Lard to be his servant

when he's only 16 years old
met his lovely wife that same summer
my mama sez she figgered he's right
all boys that age get calt
some of them even on the telephone
but she thought the Lard
got a wrong number that time
we all scrut up now and then

he had about 9 kids
sed it was the Lard's will
oldest one not even 12
his wife looked like a inner tube
without about ½ its air
you'd hear her in the grocery store
2 aisles over
her feet drug so
she's wore out not even 30
and known it was her
before you saw her
by the sound

even if he got his preacher pay
and a house and a car
and his electric and water
with all them kids he thought
it wasn't enough to get by on
ever 3d Sunday the sermon
was on the collection plate
and the bread on the water
he'd go round town
asking all the business for a preacher discount
wouldn't buy nothing in a store
if they didn't mark it down for him
when they didn't
he could make them sorry for it

he'd find some way to get it
into one of his sermons
whole churchhouse would go
somewheres else after that
whether they believed it or not
his kids got in the pitchershow
½ price and free meals
at the school lunchroom
and the ball games without paying
because it was the Lard's will

so oncet he went to Lela's cafe
for supper with his whole family
stood there at the counter
before he'd set down
sed how much is your menstral discount
to eat there
customers listening, 2 waiting to pay
sez I need at least 20 percent?
Lela sed whar? she wasn't even
a Baptist but a Presbyter
sez my family and I get discounts
because of I'm the Baptist Reverent
of up to ½ at most places
one of the people eating there
Clovis Robinson I think
sed yesma'am that's a fact
he's a Baptist deacon
had to back him up without no choice
wasn't nothing she could do
everbody watching to see
if they'd all walk out
Lela sed set down
I'll do my 20 percent one time
all them kids standing there

with their mouths hanging open
3 of them didn't even
have their britches zipped up

he order tunafish sandwitches
and a glass of water
for all them kids because it was cheapest
fried chicken for his wife
because that was most for the money
and told this waitress
to bring him a steak to eat
how do you want that cooked? she sed
Scriptural he sed
she sed what?
he sez well done
my good and faithful servant
leant back and grint
proud of hisself like he thought
she ought to brang him a dish of icecream
for free for thinking that up

Lela heard it
hollered through the winder
from the cash register to the cook
whole cafe listening
fix that preacher's kids hamburgers
with french fries
make his wife shrimps and whitefish
put him a steak on
from off the bottom of the pile
I'll pay the different
cook sez how he want that steak?
she yelled Scriptural
burn that sonofabitch to hell
he never did come back there

to eat again after that
and it never hurt Lela's business
not even one bit

Deaf

Clovis Walker had this uncle
by marriage who went deaf
when he was about 40
they sed it was shooting firecrackers
when he's a boy out of season
but he sed they lied
he only did it July too
except for that one year
when they fount them blasting caps
it run in his family
his daddy couldn't hear neither

when he's 52
he was feeding his sow with pigs
she whirlt round and bit
half his hand off
where he had a thumb
and 2 fingers left
she swallered the rest
he sed he seen her smacking
her lips on it
couldn't hear a thang
he always wondered
if he could of heard
mebbe he'd known she's gone
bite him off like that
grunting loud to scare him off
but it wasn't no warning for him

so he was in his 60's
forgot anybody else

could hear either
he'd set in his chair at night
by the fireplace staring at it
listening backwards to hisself
rub that hand and say out loud
that goddam sow. That goddam sow

Doc

Doc Kitchens told me
about this trapper he took the appendix out of
name Robb Valton
the one got his finger cut off
but he found it
put it in his pocket
when he got home
sewed it back on the stump part
didn't work
fell off after a week
so he buried it
but his dog smelt it
and dug it up
had it on the porch that night
green gnawing on it
sed he kicked that dog
all the way under his truck
off that porch
it turnt his stomach

so before that
when he's younger
before he even had a truck
he's up in the hills
working his lines
got this bellyache
so bad he couldn't stand up
had to crawl back
thought he'd die for sure
but it was a miracle
some 12 year old boys

up there in his line shack
broke in looking for stills
to steal sugar from and sell
and mebbe some whiskey
they could get drunk on
or if it was bad
go blind and be famous
he caught them in there
blocked off the door
sed I'll kill you right now
and make a lampshade
out the skin off your butt
or one of you can go get Doc Kitchens
and tell him I'm bad off
while the otherns stay here till dark
and then I'll kill you anyway
if whichevern's not back by then

they commenced to bellering
so bad he sed
get out of here right now
I caint stand that
but one of you tell Doc
I need help
and if you don't I'll find you in the night
that's a fact

they's scairt
run all the way to town
2 of them bawled the whole way
thought he's follering
but the othern did what he sed

Doc Kitchens sed
is it sumin busted?

boy sez I don't think so
he stood up and wave his arms
Is it snakebite?
No he wasn't slobbering
Was it blood?
No I never seen none
Damn he's poisoned
or the kidney stone he sed
and I only got 2 bottles of whiskey
he saddled his horse
took off

Robb Valton he's laying on the floor
in a bunch when Doc Kitchens got there
hollering oh I'm gone die
Doc sez sit up so I can see what's wrong
sed oh I'm gone die
sez sit up goddammit
or I'll whup your ast with a board
he got up and set on the table
Doc did a examination and sez
by god you got the appendicitis
Robb Valton sez is it any pills
I can take for it?
Doc sez no I'm gone have
to operate and get her out
Oh I'm gone die he said

Doc sed he sez here
you take and drink this
fast as you can
give him one bottle of whiskey
started boiling the water
got in the drawer and pulled out
all the knives

set down on the furniture
with a whetstone
started sharpening

Robb Valton drank that bottle
but couldn't get drunk
sed isn't it no more whiskey?
Doc sez here you do this
you're bettern I am at it
given him the knives to get sharp
he went to get the othern

they sharpened and Robb Valton drank
until he finally stopped and sed
you gone use these on me?
Doc sez yes I am
and the duller it is
the more you gone feel it
he sed in about 2 minutes
them knives was sharp enough
to shave a porcupine
and Robb Valton looked drunk
so he sed lay down on the table
and take your pants off

tied him down with a rope
top to bottom where only his head could move
sed try to go to sleep
so you won't feel nothing
that knife was sharp
had him open in a second
and a half looking for it
about had a spasm
sed he couldn't find that appendix
in there nowhere
he got scairt wondered

if he'd cut the hole on the wrong side
and if he made 2 holes
Robb Valton would kill him
the next day for sure
he was as big as a boar hog
drunk or not
Robb Valton he lifted up his head
sed you cut me yet?
Doc sez no just shaving the hair off
he sed then let me up 1st
I gotta pee
Doc sez oh it's too late for that
I's lying you're open
he sed oh god I'm gone die
hollered, pissed all over the table
then like a ruptured volcano
puked straight up in the air
hollering at the same time
oh god I'm gone die
covered the walls and floor

Doc sed it was like
a stick of dynamite went off
in a rope factory
it was guts come spewing
out that hole everwhere
sed he's grabbing with both hands
and had his knee up on his chest
trying to hold them all down
wished he'd been borned a octopus
intestines wallering all over
Robb Valton bawling yelling
oh I'm gone die then puking
straight up in front of him
right there it was
that appendix all green

sticking up like a thumb
he grapt it and had it down
on the table and off
then had to get it all
shoved back in
sed he never imagined a elephant
had that many in there
but Robb Valton helped by passing out
he sewed him up
didn't even have a shot to give him

put the appendix
in a mason jar of whiskey to keep
so he could take it home
to put on a shelf and look at
had him a drink
and went to sleep
setting up in a chair watching
to see if he'd die

sed 1st thing he remembered
was Robb Valton shaking him
arredy had coffee on
sez you sonofabitch
you sewed some scissors or pliers
up inside me
it's summin in there hurts
never would tell him
how he got untied from that table

sed for years
ever time he'd see him
Robb Valton'd pull his pants down
and show where Doc Kitchens
cut him open with a axe

and sewed him up with baliwore
ever kid in town seen that scar

he's the only doctor we had
and got his degree out the back
of a funny book they sed
until they built the hospital
and got a real one
he had to retire
and go to horses and dogs
in the shed behind his house
but Mama told me
he was the 1st person to slap my ast
so I figger he must of
been worth something
I known Robb Valton
sed he'd of been dead many a time
if it wasn't for Doc Kitchens
but he sure as hell wished
he'd of been there
when he needed him for that finger

Bryant Williamson

Onriest man in town I guess
was old Bryant Williamson the 1st
that was his boy's and
his boy's name too the 2nd and 3d
in a row with the same name
he's rich
made his seed money in the oil
off his ranch

he put part of that oilmoney
in a insurance business
he had a brother in the goverment
known what was coming up
how the goverment was gone make
everybody buy the insurance
he got in
before it caught on
was a millionaire back then
when it was worth something
from the oil and the insurance both

he's smart and sent them boys
to school to be lawyers
teach the people
how to sue each other
so he could sell more insurance
when they got sued for protection
had the law office right there
the insurance next to it
with a door in between
and a doorbell on both

so one of them could run it
at a time and the rest could be
doing something else
everything they did made money

after he's rich he didn't care
what nobody thought
he had enough money to mind
whoever's business he wanted to
or not his own if he felt like that
whatever's on his mind
didn't stay in it he sed it out loud

once the radio station called him
sez is this Bryant Williamson?
he sed who the hell
you think it is? you called me
I never touched the telephone till it rung
radio sez Mr. Williamson
you on the air
he sed is that a fact?
radio sez yas and the reason
we calling is you just bought
a new Ford from Ed Power Fordhouse
and we want you to tell
the listening public in your own words
how much you appreciate
that new Ford from Ed Power's

he sed in my own words
that is the sorriest goddam
piece of machinery anybody
ever put on a set of wheels
since they invented Mack trucks
I'm thinking about
putting one of Charley Baker's idiots

in it and driving it off a cliff
saying he stoled it for the insurance
I wouldn't drive that thing
to a dam goatroping contest
and if somebody wants to take Ed Power
out and shoot him in the head
I'll buy the bullet
he's one lying cheap snotnose sonofabitch
you can quote me in the newspaper
I'll buy the advertisement

it was a highschool boy
running the radiostation that day
following orders
didn't know how
to turn him off
it went on the radio
we all heard it except Ed Power we guessed
he never sued him
we thought for sure he would
but he wouldn't of won
the only lawyers that was suers
was Williamsons then

he had to go to the doctor
for a specialist up to the capital once
his boy the 2nd drove him
they went by the college on the way
at this stoplight
college boy in a red car
that looked like a football player
pulled up beside him
Bryant Williamson leaned out
and spit Brown Garrett snuff all on his face
in his red car with the top down
that boy jumped out

would of put dents on his head
but Bryant Junior the 2nd
run over and stopped him
sed look we sorry
he's a old man you can see that
look at him he never meant that
it was a accident
here take this handkerchief of mine
it's a new one cost 2 dollars
you wipe that off and keep it
it's yours you don't owe me nothing
that boy calmed down
sed all right but I don't like that
one bit you better get him out of here
Bryant the 2nd sed I am
I'm taking him to the doctor
right now he don't see too good
that's what's the matter

he got back in
old man Williamson sed
the sonofabitch should of
had his winder rolt up
before that boy could get out
Bryant pulled in the off lane
run the red light and turned left
on a one way street wrong
honking his horn to get away
he wasn't gone have nobody
whup his ast over that

so when he died
they read his will it sed
I caint take my money with me
but I can take my fish
he wouldn't let nobody fish

on his place
him and Beulah K. Byrd
had a advertisement in every Thursday paper
no hunting fishing or trespassing
on my ranch signed their name
Beulah on hers had
survivors will be persecuted by the law
she drove around in a jeep
with a 410 shotgun looking for you
she'd shoot if she seen you
on her land but Williamson
hired a Mexican to look for him
so after they buried him
they went to all his stocktanks
thrown 3 sticks of dynamite in it
every one and killed all the fish
by god just to show he could do
whatever he wanted to
with anything that was his

Clean

Are your garments spotless,
are they white as snow,
are you washed in the blood of the Lamb?
CHRISTIAN HYMNAL NUMBER TWO

Cleanest woman that ever lived
was Mizrez Bullard
her kids' ears bled she scrubbed so hard
even on Wednesday night prayer meeting
and after she washed clothes
in her house on Thursday
she'd use the washing machine water
to mop the porch and the sidewalk
and the street curb all clean

then her husband before he ran off
brought home this white cat
for the kids he named Nookie
so after she did those clothes and sheets
on Thursdays she's so clean
she washed that cat

it never went out of the house
but on Thursdays when she got out
the washing machine
you could see it through the window
trying to scratch a hole out
then by afternoon when she's finishing clothes
it'd be a white streak
across the floor one room to another

every one of her kids ran off and left
before they got out of school

and her husband with another woman
she still washed everything in the house
every Thursday and that cat
it wasn't no chance for it to get away
she had one thing on her mind
and anything it was dirty
didn't have no place in there to hide

you'd hear her looking for it
hollering here Nookie Nookie, come here kitty
a block away you'd know
when she found it hiding by the squall
her arms had scratch marks
all the way up but she never felt a thing
by god, her and that cat was clean

Barbed Wire

You just cut that sombitch
right here
KARL POPP, *Yarbrough Mountain*

It isn't no easy way
to find the endpiece of wore
oncet it's in the roll
you can pick it up bounced it round
like this or roll it
upside the barn hard
mebbe it'll pop out
most times not
don't cost nothing to try
it was this man back home
name Johnny Ray Johnston
a inventer
he invented this thing it could help
find the endpiece
and sent it off to Warshington

he had this brother
name Harold Wayne Johnston
a blind gospelpreacher
he wasn't always
he's a mean sonofabitch young
all filt up with sin and equity
fighting raising hell
had three four of them girls
his age up to the doctor
all before he's called
it was this brother
name Leonas Timothy Johnston
he never learned to read

so he got a job with the highway patrol
got shot by a shiner
I seen that worefinder
it worked my brother he bought one
where'd them pliers go?
so Harold Wayne one day
he's out in this field
where the neighbors run his hogs
hiding in the shinery
shooting a pellet gun
to watch them squolt and run
I guess he was lessee
it was two years before he tried to heal
Mavis Tittle's one that died
of the toothache so he must of been twenty-four
goddam watch it
worell tear the hide right off
your hands you seen them gloves?

this storm come up a sudden
caught him out there
looking like a cyclone
he had to get home so he run
by the time he got to the fence
it was hailballs coming down
he tried to climb through with the gun
poached hisself
shot right up his nose
made all the blood go in his eyeballs
he's blind
that fence caught him
he's straddled of one wore
the top one had him grapt by the butt
here comes the storm
he sez he could feel that wore
go green when the lightning struct

made him a eunuch
he could look right at a naked womern
wouldn't nothing go down
nor come up after that
you find them pliers? look
in the jockey box or under the seat
sez he heard God call him

he'd been hollering like a sonofabitch
they heard all the way to the house
and was fixing to come but he quit
they waited till it quit raining
sez they'd of thought he's dead
and that would of made two
only one brother left for a seed crop
all that blood out his nose
except he's praying to hisself out loud
he never even heard them come up
it isn't none there? look
in the back see if it's some sidecutters
or something so they known he'd got religion
and they never seen he's even blind yet

he's a gospelpreacher after
and Johnny Ray's a inventer
Leonas Timothy was arredy shot dead
what it was was a piece of wore
it could be fixed on the end at the store
except it was red paint on it
wherever the red was was the end
when you's through using wore
then fix the red one on
next time there'd be the endpiece red
Harold Wayne he saved hundreds of lostsouls
come all over to hear him heal
best on headaches and biliousness

it was this one family had this crippled boy
come about eighty miles to see him gospelpreach
brung this boy up front
he taken and grapt his head
hollers the words and sez now walk
but he fell on his ast still crippled
they sez it wasn't Harold Wayne's fault
them people didn't have faith
I heard he drownt a year or two after that

the goverment never did send Johnny Ray
no patent agreement we figgered
he kept the invention for hisself
so Johnny Ray he made some up
and sold to his friends around town
you caint buy it nowhere else
I wisht I had one now
I've waste more damn time on wore today
than I have to lose
bring them pliers here
let's cut this sonofabitch it don't matter where
we gone set here all day
won't never get this damn fence done

Faith Tittle

HEBREWS 11:1-3

John, I said, have you
ever spayed a gilt?
What'd you say? sez John
I said castrated a female pig
it's called spaying.
I known that
I known what spading is
I just caint figger out
why you asking

It was this Ag teacher
back home I remember
who wanted to be a vet sed John
he didn't make it neither
so he did the next best
he liked to try
all them fancy operations
he's good on ruptures
and worms and even
untwisted a horse's gut oncet
I heard and cows' eyes
he castarated a bunch of chicken
made them capers he sez
sed they'd grow fancy feathers
and get fat and sell
for a lot of money
but they all died first
and he cut some girl pigs
spaded them up
most of them died too
nobody known if it was his fault

the ones that lived
was just like barrows
ate and got fat and never come in
It was this one womern
in town we called Faith Tittle
back then cause it was her name
call her Judy after that I heard
that was real fat
she couldn't lose no weight
if she tried so she taken and went
to the doctor and he give her
thyroid pills and diets
and examinations
finally he sez she has to have
a hystericalalectomy for womern
they gone take all her female parts out
and then mebbe she wouldn't be so fat
Doctor told her, Faith Tittle
it's something inside I caint see
some substance I just hope
I can get rid of for you
and then you'll be better off

Faith Tittle wasn't sure
she'd do that cause that doctor
he'd been a Baptist
medical missionary, he played
piano music in his office
and she's a Campbellite
she couldn't trust him for sure
so she went down to anothern
to see what he thought
and he played band music
in his office and was a Methodist
so when he sed yas
she ought to have it all took out

she wasn't married anyway
and was arredy over thirty
wasn't doing her no good
she figgered he'd believe anything
and probley change his mind
about it at the same time
so she sed she wanted to go off
by herself and work it out
where there wasn't no music
playing because that one doctor
he sed we better take out
the whole works and she's afraid
without that she's about as good
as dead and was it worth it

She went to her kinfolk
Leonard Tittle, he's a Campbellite preacher
I don't know what kin he was
he'd been a algebrar teacher
at the high school but his breath
was too bad, the kids couldn't stand it
when he leant over to help
with their homework
they'd of rather failt than had him help
so he had to finally find
something else to do
that he could be good at mebbe
so he took to preaching
at the Lorenzo ChurchofChrist
she sed she didn't know what to do
he told her some Methodists
and Baptists wasn't all bad
they might not go to heaven
but they could do operations
on earth okay and he'd pray
it'd probley work out

so she done it
they cut her open
both doctors was there at the same time
hauled off a wheelbarrow load
of stuff come out of her they sed
that operation wasn't no more
than sewed back up
news was all over town
from the nurses and doctors and wives
they found knots of flesh
and hair and a set of teeth
inside her womb growing there
they didn't know how long
and lumps the size of a cantaloupe
down to a golfball
took it all out and thrown it
in the trashcan
except the hair and teeth they sed
it got put in a jar and sent off
to Warshington to see what it was

She's ruint
all over town they's talking about it
her business was everbody's
and down in the flats
they's scairt to death of her
say her name out loud
their eyes swelt up like a coffeecup
they sez she been with the devil
you could pull out a wad of doghair
they'd have a spasm
thinking it might be her hairball
I'd of love to had a set
of falseteeth back then
but I never

Faith Tittle had to leave
it wasn't nothing there
for her no more
she went before the Campbellite church
and asked to be prayed for
with the rest of the sick and afflicted
then she changed her name to Judy
they sed and left
dunno whar she went
it don't matter, Leonard Tittle
stood up in the churchhouse
sed all things wake to the good
for those which love the Lard
and he's her kinfolk
so I spoze she come out okay
wherever she went
to start over again

But no
I never done one, have you?
What? I said.
Spaded no girlpig
what are you talking about?
I just cain't see no advantage
if the boar stays in his pen
where he's posta be
until it's time to turn him in
they eat the same as any hog
either way just the same
so what's the different
why take a chanct
if you ain't sure
what you're doing?

Fast

Janie Grace Gosset could outrun anybody
in the high school back then
before she had that car wreck
if she'd of been borned a boy
she could of been on the football team
except she's probley too little
her whole body was one piece of muscle
like a carpenter's crowbar
welded together without even a joint
you could of struct a match on her
you don't believe me?
a gopher match, anywhere

she'd wear bluejeans to the school on Fridays
like all the girls did oncet
it look like two boar hogs in there
fighting it out in a chicken coop
when she walked past you with them britches on
Edgar McMahon down to the gin
sed if he could get cotton that tight
he'd put a 800 pound bale in a tow sack

then she took up with that sorry Harold Wayne Johnston
before he went blind and started being a gospelpreacher
he slobbered all over her
for about a half a year
until he ruint her reputation so he'd have a excuse
to move on to anothern
they sed she's going 80 miles a hour at least
when she went off the caprock
after he done it all and told

it was this one springtime
they's having the highschool track meet
whole town come out to see
if she could outrun Jimmy Ray Gary
who was gone graduate and go to the college
be on the team there
they had all the other races first
so we'd have to wait and see
finally it come to the last one
there she was in it
wearing this tight pink running outfit

that gun went off
first half she was out in front good
then he pulled up, all the otherns
was done behind by then
them two right beside each other the last part
everbody there was struck deaf and dumb
like they's on the road to Damascus
their mouths hanging open like it was a vision
for just a second or 2 that day turned into pear jelly
her body melted into that running suit
looked like she was bald naked running wide open
only one othern seemed to be moving
besides them 2 was Harold Wayne Johnston
running down to the finish line to grab her
like she's a Holstein cow right in front of everbody
probley thought she done all that just for him

I don't think anybody could tell you
who won that footrace
we lost that in the watching
but we all had words for it
that we known by heart
I heard my mouth say Amazing Grace
we all remember R.B. McCravey hollering

that there's poetry in motion
Ollie McDougald sed it was a religious experience
but Leonard Tittle who was already preaching on
    weekends
and had both of them in his class of algebrar
sez right out loud
nosir gentlemen you are all wrong
that was Grace abounding to the chief of sinners

Potts Coal Mine, Inc.

Brother Coy Stribling
finally got this job
working in the coal mine
he'd been fired
from everything else
except preaching at the Church of God
that believed in flags
didn't make enough
to get by on
he'd about hit bottom
when he got hired

hadn't been working there
a week when it was a cave-in
right when he was telling them
about the Ethiopian eunuch
about a half mile down
felt the mountain shake
heard it grunt
they run back up
it's closed off
sealt in

stood there a minute
staring at that slide rock
Coy Stribling sez
brethern let us pray
he started the preacher prayer
nobody could understand
about the mysteries of the Lard

and the faith in the churchhouse
Jimmy Don McCampbell sed
goddam I smell gas
let's dig
all them miners took after
that rock pile
like a chainsaw
slinging it everywhere

Coy Stribling he seen
finally it wasn't nobody listening
so he gave it up
and even he started digging
some said it was only time
anybody ever seen him
turn a hand
they's scairt
nobody down there thought
they might not
get out of that one dead

dug till some of them
was bleeding up both arms
some bawling
others hollering
to keep them all working
never known how long
they'd been at it
batteries in their headlights run out
it wasn't no time down there
dark as Jonah's whale
and then they broke through

it was a little hole
but they could smell the air

and known if they messed with it
whole thing might cave in
they took a chance
one at a time crawlt through
skinny ones 1st
fat ones ready for Brother Coy
to stop preaching
about the camel's eye and the needle
but they didn't have to tell him
ever one of them made it
through that hole
him 3d from last
some had scrape marks on their ribs
looked like a hog fight
but they's through and running

got up that tunnel and out
no moren set down
to get a count
that mountain farted
squat down and took a shit
mud and gas and rocks
come out that hole
like a tornado's tearing out
but no fire
thrown rock
over half a mile
down the canyon
knocked ever one of them
ast over appetite
and Junior Bechamp busted his arm
didn't even know it
till the next day
but not one of them
got killed

Coy Stribling
when it was through
all settled down
and they saw they's all alive
stood up and sed
would you like to sing a hymn, brethern?
R.B. McCravey sed
would you shut the fuck up, Coy?
he set down
never said another word

They's there for a hour
in the night
nobody moving or saying nothing
waiting for morning
when the rescue party come up
from town to find the bodies
they'd heard the blow up
known everbody in that mine was dead
walked right up on them
without seeing them setting there
J.R. Potts sez whar's the mine
I caint see it?
Jimmy Don McCampbell sed
it's right over there but it's sealt off
J.R. Potts about died
of the heart attack
he sez goddam you
you like to scairt me to death
where are you?
and they shined the light on them
you posta be all dead he sed
how come you setting round like that?
Coy Stribling sed we watching
in the garden
with the Lard, brother

R.B. McCravey was ready to kill him
but he just sed kiss my ast, Coy

they opened that mine
back up in one week
almost everbody
who was in there that day
went back to work
except for a couple and
Coy Stribling
he sed he'd seen enough
he'd find something else to do
after that and he
wouldn't never get inside no hole again
as long as he lived
and his wife sed bless the Lard
for that at least
he sed not in the ground
until they buriet me
and she sed oh that
got a job at the grocery store

they cleared out all that rock
put in new timber
and had her bored and stroked
to the end in 2 months
back on schedule
J.R. Potts sed that mine was as safe
as a schoolhouse
he'd certify so hisself
and all them men sed
the mountain felt settled down
like she'd got rid
of whatall's on her mind
they didn't have no more troubles
or a accident

for almost a year after that
everbody figured
it might of been worth it
to get him that job
at the grocery store

Lazy

Laziest man ever was Floyd Scott
it wasn't nothing that boy
would ever do for anybody
when he's 5 years old
arredy too late his mama one day
sez Floyd come take this trash out
to the barrel but he just lain there
in the living room on the furniture
so she sez you taking this trash out
like I told you?
he never answered she sed
you want to take this trash out
to the barrel or do you want a whipping?
he sez finally how many licks?
she sed 3 with the flyswatter
he didn't say nothing for a minute
she thought he's coming to get it
then he sed do I have to
come out there or will you come
give it to me in here?

When he's about 12
they had supper one night called him
to come set down at the table to eat
he sed he wasn't hungry yet
they sed you don't have to eat then
he sed he was arredy there
he might as well wait till he felt like it
set there 3 hours with his elbows
on the table waiting to get hungry
they hadn't put their winderscreens

up yet and it was hot, winders open
his mama come to check on him
his face swolt up like a pomegranate
mosquitos eat him up
couldn't even closed his mouth
had 3 mosquito bites on his tongue
too lazy to get up and move
he sed it was their fault
he calt for somebody to come close that winder
they had the television up so loud
he couldn't holler above it
it wasn't polite to get up
from the table before he's through eating

got him a job with his in-laws
where they couldn't fire him cause he's family
he wasn't worth a dam
tried to get him to string fencewore
left him there one morning
they come back to get him for dinner
he's still standing there with his hands
in his pockets staring at that wore
come up and touch him on the shoulder
he jumped straight up with his eyes open
sez goddam you snuck up on me
when I's studying how to unroll
all that wore out straight for 4 hours
give him a shovel to dig with
he leaned on it till he had a dent under his chin
had to go to the doctor to see
if the bottom of his tongue ruptured
for years when they wanted a shovel
they'd say brang me Floyd's dragline here

had to promote him to a desk job
for setting a bad influence on the other hired hands

give him the job of making coffee and answering
    telephone
he wouldn't even do that
his mama'd bring him to work and make it for him
had to buy a answering machine
he sed ever time it rung he was always busy
checking the coffee or setting in the toilet

he was 24 years old when he
went and got in the car to drive
down to the grocery store a block away
to get him a can of beer
had this terrible itch that was a tragedy
he stretched up to scratch his ast
hit the curb and rolled the car
on flat ground right over
Doctor sed he couldn't find
nothing wrong with the x-ray
but his back wasn't strong enough
for him to walk on it after that
insurance bought him 4 different wheelchairs
all too hard for him to use
till they got one with a electric motor on it
he sed he was satisfied
never walked a hundred steps in a row after that
some days he sed it was too hard and not worth the effort
to even get out of bed to it
so he got a television set in his bedroom
to help him get by on social security
that same year 4 kinds of welfare
and the Assemblyofgod brought his supper
on all days with a R in them

county paid for him a private nurse
because he sed it was a soft spot
in that pavement caused his accident

of their negligence and behavior
he was gone sue the county
and the town for a million dollars
if they didn't take care of him till he got well
they thought it'd be cheaper to buy him a nurse
for however long it took
after 3 years she found a way to get married to him
and still have the county pay her for being a nurse's helper
bought them a trailerhouse they put in
right next to his daddy's house
where he didn't have to pay no rent
after that she give up her other patients
and kept the county money for watching him
it was enough to get by on they sed

she's almost as lazy as he was
I heard moss grown in her toilets
they put a deep freezer out on the front porch
to hold the TV dinners she fixed
on all days without a R
both of them got so fat they had to have 2 couches
in the living room to set and watch TV on
so lazy a dog couldn't live with them
it'd of starved to death waiting
for one of them to come feed it

The Sawmill Road

We got our town supply
of cripples on the sawmill road
it wasn't a year or a season
went by that somebody didn't get
mashed up one way or anothern
on that road

it started about a mile
out of town and went straight up
to blowup where the 1st sawmill was
and the boiler exploded years ago
killing 2 men and one
they never found
either blowed all to hell
or left without sending word
it's not a flat place on that road
yougn speak of anywhere
hard going up or down
and dangerous
a lot of people got killed
and their bones busted
on the sawmill road

back then when wagons
was what we had
it was always a runaway
or a accident about to happen
somebody got ruint for life
Charlie Ivie was coming
downhill loaded with 2 ton of cutwood
for a barn when his neck yoke busted

wagon rode up on the horses
pushed them ahead of it
going straight down
and this drag he made
out of some logs he chained up
to the back
to slow it down come loose
his brakes wouldn't hold
wagon pushed the horses
off the road heading right for a cliff
Charlie Ivie give it up
jumped off but caught his foot
in the brakerope
it throwed him under
crushed his legs
where one had to be cut off
other one wouldn't bend
he's a sorry dam mess from then on
but the wagon turned on its own
the horses wasn't killed
they saved the wood
but he had to sell it
he couldn't build no barn after that

Ray Evans's daddy took a load
uphill to sell it to the mill
he had Ray with him
he's about 14 back then
horse stumbled
wagon started to roll back
so his daddy yelled
jump down off them logs where he's setting
and block off the wheel
Ray couldn't find no rock close by
quick so he shoved his food under
he sed he wouldn't do that again

mashed it flat like a duck
waddled like a fat womern
on that side from then on

the one we's all scared of
got Clarence Murphy
the pole strap that fits
over the neck yoke fastened
to the britchens on the harness
to keep the wagon from rolling ahead
and for backing it up
finally broke
and his brakes wouldn't hold
he jumped and got tangled
wagon went over his chest
left him splattered all over the road
turned sideways and rolled
killed one horse and broke the othern
he had to be shot
nobody got crippled though
they had to get him all in a cotton sack
to bring him down

it was right below that place
my brother and me
found that branch
and the still where
he got his finger chopped off
in the leaf springs of a wagon
stealing sugar
but it didn't make him no cripple

my uncle Elwood was going up
tandem with Cletus Young
to the sawmill when he seen
this waspnest hanging on a tree limb

he got up and crawled back
along the reach and whacked it
with a axe handle
whipped them horses with a rein
for a ways and pulled off
the side the road
here comes Cletus Young standing up
on the double tree of his wagon
them horses running belly to the ground
with a string of wasps following
like he's dragging a plow
went right on past
when he outrun them he come back
hit my uncle Elwood oncet
so hard he's knocked out
busted 2 teeth but he sed
it was worth it
Cletus got stung in his ear
sed it got him down deep
and he couldn't hear out of it no more
but we never believed him

had a lot of hunting accidents
on that road where we'd go
for turkeys and deer
R.B. McCravey's one boy was hunting
on his horse with R.B.'s rifle
without permission
this deer run out
he had that rifle in his lap
lifted it up and fired too fast
without sighting he shot
that horse in the back of his head
when it fell down it trapped him
his one leg broke
where he limped from then on

and his hand with the rifle in it
was under him and the horse
and the saddle
smashed it up where it never did
work right after that
he wore a glove on it
couldn't even hold a cigarette
or write his name

Cephas Bilberry was hunting
rabbits up there
when he thought he seen
these turkeys out of season
he climbt through this fence
to get them and poached hisself
shot off half his chin and part of his face
a handful of teeth and one eye
on that side
he walked down that mountain
all the way home
sed he was afraid he might of
bled to death
but it never got a good start
figured mebbe the heat off the shotgun
sealed it off shut
he was a sight after that
couldn't even let him
pass the plate
the contribution would go down
ever Sunday he did

after we started driving cars
it was about a wreck a month
at 1st till we got used to it
then down to a few every year
some dead

like the Clarys that went off
Left Hand Canyon
or old man Benson that run
into a logging truck
he was too old to drive
should of known better

when he's young
before he got blinded by lightning
Harold Wayne Johnston was up there
on a Saturday night
in the back seat with Marva Beth Williamson
the hand brake must of slipped
or they got to rocking
it come out of gear
that car rolled a quarter of a mile backwards
hit a tree and broke her back
she's so skinny she could of
walked up to a flagpole
and bit a piece off
without turning her head sideways
so it might not of hit that hard
Harold Wayne sed he never known
a thing till it hit
sed he was amazed by it all
she's paralyzed for a while
but got better
walked like a goose from then on
but she's so skinny
we never noticed it
we didn't look at her that much

there's not a foot of that road
don't remember somebody by name
Carla Prowst got 5 unmarried kids up there
named every one

after its daddy
we lost a banker and a Baptist deacon
and a deputy sheriff over that road
every time she went up
we'd watch to see
who left town

when the ambulance come from that direction
we known it was a bad one
we'd wait a day to see
if Edna Mae worn her golden shoes
then we'd call the hospital
to see who and how bad
the whole town got infected
by that road
it wasn't hardly nobody
man or womern who grew up there
who didn't lose something sometime
on the Sawmill Road
we even wondered once
if we oughta close it off
but the town board decided if we didn't have
our Sawmill Road cripples
we'd be too perfect
and that's a load
that's too heavy to carry

No Lazy S Ranch

1

KEEP OUT
NO TRASSPASSING
POSTED
DONT COME
KEEP THIS GOD DAM GATE CLOSE

2

Kay Stokes had more money than God
he had this one grandboy
that was the football player
went on to the college to do it
in high school
man sed he had to take this class
in algebrar from Leonard Tittle
before he was being a preacher
his breath was too bad
that Patrick boy was too rich
to have that in his ear
if he needed help
it would hang there
you'd have to go to the bathroom
warsh that smell off
so he sed no he wouldn't
he could arredy count to 800
that was enuf to count his oilwells
and on a good day
all 4,000 cows on the No Lazy S Ranch
he didn't need no algebrar

and Kay Stokes sed if he did
he'd buy him one to do it
he could play some football
besides having money
and ordering people around
and making sure nobody
ever set foot on his private property
without his permission which he wouldn't give
to the President of the United States
or the Catholic Pope if he was a Englishman
the only thing he ever took a inarrest in
was watching that boy play football
he offered to buy some professionals
to come play on that team for him
high school wouldn't let him
sed it was against the rules
he went to the school board
to get them to fire the principal
because the football coach
sed it might be a good idear
if he was willing to do it

didn't work
they sed he didn't need to
that team was gone win all its games
without no illegal help or otherwise
sed they's afraid the stands would cave in
so many people would come
watch that boy
Kay Stokes had this other idear
paid the money to have this fence
built all around the football field
6 foot high with barbwore on top
to make sure everbody paid to get in
he sed it wasn't no white trash
or otherns gone watch that boy play

without buying no ticket
he'd see to that at least
school make enough money
selling football tickets to build a addition
on the Superintendent's house
and buy the football coach
a new car
so it was worth it they sed

school taken and given
him a celebration to thank him
for that fence that sold all them tickets
made him a sign
to go on the wall with his name on it
in a picture frame
had a assembly with all the kids there
and the teachers and the parents
and the Superintendent and the football coach
and the 1st Christianchurch preacher
about 9 speeches telling the world
what a fine rich man he was
and a churchhouse prayer to thank Godamighty
for Kay Stokes
that grandboy up on the stage with him
then asked him if he wanted
to speak a few words for the occasion

he set there staring
for a minute
stood up and sed it's 2 things
I have to say
number one I accept this here award
on behalf of Jesus Christ
and the No Lazy S Ranch
and number 2
I bought me a Mexican

it caint read or hardly speak no language
to drive round the fences
on my ranch and I sed to shoot
on sight anybody traspassing on my property
after first making sure it aint me
or has my written permission
which it caint read
so if you aint my twin brother
keep your ast off my land
you want to fish
you go see that sonofabitch Bryant Williamson
he aint done one dam thing
for this town
not one of his kids
could be on that football team
you tell him I sed so
he set down and waited for them to clap
so that's what they did

3

his hired hands
would of rather had the burning bush
tell them they castarated the wrong bull
than have Kay Stokes get out the rag on them
his word was the Law
and if he fired them they might as well
leave the country
if they committed suicide
wouldn't nobody bury them
they'd feed them to Wesley Stevens's hogs

oncet he seen these 2 setting down
snuck up behind them
to hear if they's saying something about him
but they's on wormen that day

saved their life probley
sed I suspicion you boys
done need something to do
one couldn't say nothing he's so suprized
othern sez yessir that's just what
we was getting ready to talk about
he sed you both of you go get a shovel
and right out there beside the road
where I can see you
start digging a hole
until I say stop
he known 2 foot down
they'd hit some caliche
like digging through a Republican's opinions
he went to town in his pickup

forgot them boys
he didn't come back
till the next afternoon
they had this hole 12 foot deep
taking turns digging
the othernd haul the dirt up
with a bucket on a rope
one couldn't swim
he's praying they didn't hit no water
othern was saying
just kick your legs
stay on top if it comes
I'll try to get a rope on you
make sure your head don't get down
you'll drownd for sure
othern's so worried he's sweating
and they'd got through
being tored a long time ago
Kay Stokes pulled up
looked in that hole

sed that's about good
go 9 more inches and then
do one on the other side
the same size
drove right on by
one hired hand had to wrap his hand up
in his handkerchief
blisters done all broke
they hadn't even stopped
to have no breakfast or supper
they's so ascaired of him

called California on the telephone
they mailed him 2 redwood trees
put them in them holes for gateposts
and a board acrost the top for a marker
about 40 foot high
sez No Lazy S Ranch
No hunting or fishing by permission only
You Aint Welcome

4

he put him up a fence
running 2 miles straight
out of fenceposts cut off the limbs
of boardarc trees
when it rained them boardarc fenceposts
come alive and started being trees
almost ever one of them grown up
he sed he believed that must of been
the tree in the Garden of Eden
preacher sed no
that tree had a apple in it in the Bible
Kay Stokes sez that's what happens
when you aint got no good help

they caint even get the story
wrote down the way it happened
like anybody with common sense could see
he called the elders in
they fired that preacher
they all sed they didn't think
he wasn't no good neither
it was time for him to leave
it didn't matter
he bought them anothern

5

he had a heart attack
so bad it busted out both his eardrums
and his eyes bugged out
worse than Eugene Cummings
when he died in his pigpens
doctor told his wife
it wasn't nothing he could of done
if he'd been standing there
with a shot needle in both hands
he imagined he never felt a thing
but she sed she imagined he did
he sed he was tired of the drought
it hadn't rained in a year
had to haul the cattle water
and the fish tanks dried up
so nobody was even trying to get them
wasn't even no poachers to worry about
he sed he didn't even care
about ranching no more
if it wasn't gone rain
he'd lost the taste
unless he could figure out
something to do about it

2 days after his funeral
it started to rain
they sed and there's some
who'll swear on this by god
on the 3d day of rain
in the one stock tank
over to the blue gate
it was this catfish
looked like 4 pounds
wallering in that tank
wasn't enough water to cover it up
come up through the mud
where it'd buried itself waiting
some sed it was a miracle
Mizrez Stokes sed she didn't
find it surprising at all

6

year later some people
from the town had this petition
to have the family take down
them signs and open up
the No Lazy S Ranch to public fishing
brought it to Ruby Patrick's house
which is his daughter
to give to Mizrez Stokes

she sed as long as it is one drop
of her daddy's blood
alive in anybody's veins
for as long as it takes
or that family sold that ranch
or until they could get
bananas to grow in the pastures

and teach the cows to peel them and eat them
them signs her daddy put up
would stay right there
and he promised them Mexican fenceriders
a job for life as long
as they never learnt no language
to keep all foreigners out
and it wasn't up to her
to break no promise

that was almost 30 years ago
No Lazy S hands still paint
that fence round the football field
ever year silver in the fall
all them boardarc trees are still there
and I'll bet that catfish
weighs 40 pounds
and is still alive down in that tank
because even the Lard
wasn't gone argue with Kay Stokes they sed
it had to rain right now
or he'd have to find him another job

Interlude

Help me right here sed John
and I grasped the bottom rim,
we lifted the barrel into the pickup
then sat on the tailgate, hot,
a warm canyon breeze
spilled across the yellow grass

it was this one summer back home
I's young about the time most kids
getting out of school
but I'd done quit
old man Cummings
had me heping him
lifting all this heavy weight
on a wagon load
we made a tote and set in the shade to rest
he must of started remembering
commenced to talking sez

summer clover jingle jangle

he done taken and put his hand
in his pocket and pulled out this silver dollar
looked at it like he never seen it before
smooth so you couldn't even tell
the man on the side, all the words
rubbed off from being carried so long
it was meadow clover all over
stretching out green and yellow
I didn't say nothing, he talked, sed

I was 17 they come in wagons
putting on Gypsy carnivals
whole town wanted them to go on
known they'd steal whatall's loose
everbody went to the tent that night anyway
they paid me a dollar to water horses
I worked all afternoon hard
I was 17 for a dollar

she had eyes that laughed
same color as them fancy shoes
laugh like silver bobbles
on a red and blue velvet dress
color of midnight
even in the dark I seen me
looking back from those black eyes
I wasn't scared
she shown me slow, easy
the whole field of yellow clover
bells on her shoes real soft
jingle jangle

so many nights I cant sleep
smell comes in the winder after me
when my wife's alive times
I lain the whole night beside her shaking
awake, all that dark
tearing holes in me
nothing I could do but stay there
listen for the sound of silver windbells
kids in the next room, sleeping,
nobody could smell it or hear it but me
summer clover jingle jangle

he set there staring at that money
in his hand

almost like he's talking to it
like he done forgotten
I was there too
never sed no more
put it in his pocket
and closed his eyes
I could tell he's smelling the summer grass
it was all over for then

so let's take this pigfeed
out to the pens and we'll be done
lifting it down won't be as hard
as getting it in
second half's always easier'n first

Curley

Town drunk for years
was Curley Larsen
2 years Fred Lister took over
till he ruint his liver and died
Curley got it back

he's a finish carpenter
when he felt like it
until he took his drinking serious
he'd put a door then in
it wasn't no way it looked like
you could walk through
standing up straight
he'd set there drunk monkeying
till it would close and lock

got in a terrible fight
front of the postoffice oncet with Fred
when they come for mail
sed whar you going?
othern sez what you say?
sed none of your business
well I aint ascaired of you he sez
sed prove it you sonofabitch
swung on him
standing 5 foot apart
couldn't of reached each other
with a boat paddle
swinging like a tilterwhirl

Curley hit 3 times in a row
last one all the way back
went around fell on his ast
Fred dropped down on his knees
sed I had enuf
Curley sez you win I quit
Fred puked he's breathing so hard
Curley sez I'm too old to fight you
evertime you come up
I aint doing this no more
Fred sed I'm goin home
my wife can get the damn mail
from now on if you're still here
both set in the street
almost a half hour
getting their breath back
neither one hit the othern oncet
so Curley got up finally
went off to find his car
whole crowd of people watching
went right by Mizrez Fortune
who was about 80 back then standing there
sed what you staring at you sonofabitch?
I don't know how Fred got home

he could save money
making his own beer at his house
in the garage and bathtub
he'd have a tasting party
didn't think it was polite
to drink by hisself
nobody else would much come
embarrassed of their reputation
so he'd go out back to the sheds
and drink with his pigs
specially this 1 hog

was his favorite
him and that spotted boar'd
get drunk on homemade beer
and fall down sometimes
he'd try to race him
drinking a bucket of it
but he never won

oncet drinking quart bottles
that boar'd learnt to hold it
in his mouth and tip up
like he's a man and swaller
so Curley tripped and dropt his
all spilt in the mud
he tried to get that boar's away
from him to get some of it back
before he drunk it all
you never heard such a squalling
and bellering
leggo you fat sonofabitch that's mine
I want it he hollered
that boar hung on with his teeth
squolt like you stuck him
with a icepick in the neck
Curley had to bust a board
over his head to get it away
made that hog so mad
he torn his britches leg off
trying to get it back
he'd already drunk over half

this one other time
he never come home that night
for supper or bed
next morning his wife was scairt
thought he might of died

and wrecked the car
she calt the law
looked all over and put him
on the radio to see if somebody's
found him off dead
he's out back in the hog shed
where they seen him still passed out
after dinner when they
took slops out
him and that boar drunk
laying there on top of each other
car was parked in the shade
the whole time
she never looked to see

he was making beer
in a shed out back in bottles
when he got the east wrong
sugar started working in the daylight
bottles blown all their lids off
beer spurted out on the dirt floor
they heard him in the house
hollering like he's caught hisself
in the tractor fanbelt
come out here he yelled get out here now
come running to see
if it was any blood
go get the boar he sed
get him and turn him out
he's down on his belly
slurping beer out of a dent
in the ground
hurry up and bring him goddammit
he sed it's a draining in
we caint let it all waste

Jesse

"Ugly creatures, ugly grunting creatures"
MIROSLAV HOLUB

Jesse Dixon didn't have no wife or kids
it was pigpens by his trailer outside town
he raised 200 hogs at a time instead

you'd see his beat-up pickup making rounds
filling up the barrels with his pig feed
from Jim Josey's grocery store up to town

he'd get used bread and lettuce leaves he'd need
scrounging round to make up his living out there
alone with them hogs, sagebrush and ragweed

then that damn Dickie Biggins this one year
went and found the dirtroad behind his place
took them girls out to the middle of nowhere

almost half the night on ever Friday
wallering in the backseat of his daddy's car
everbody thought it wasn't no way

somebody wouldn't have to marry his daughter
to him and ruin their lives from then on
anybody but him in the family cooky-jar

Jesse oncet in springtime seen him come round
when his sows was farreling babies in the sheds
watched that boy's car's backsprings bounce up and down

took it as long as he could they sed
went in his trailerhouse and got his shotgun
Dickie and that new girl was bare naked

when he jerked and slung that cardoor open
both thought they was about as good as dead
staring at the barrel end of that gun

"Haven't you got respect for nothing?" he sed
"you are a disgrace to the human race
Mothers and babies is in them pigsheds"

he's so pissed off tears was running down his face
screaming like a rooster when Dickie torn out
"Never bring your goddam filth back to my place"

Vera

The County Treasurer for years
was Vera Gollehans
who let cats live in the house
and had the cancer
back before it got popular
we all thought it was sumin different
that she got from having all them things
in the house with her

this one was old
whupped so many times
it didn't have no ears
on either side and a stump
for a tail looked like a Vienna sausage
when it wagged
and only one eye
it'd lain in her lap
all day at the courthouse
find its way home
jump up on the cupboard
squat and pee in the sinkhole
she sed it was so smart
but we thought it given her
the disease
we figgered it used the sink
cause it was too lazy to cover it up
it might not of been that one
she had about a dozen more
one night it was prowling
got in this ohgoddam catfight
all down the street
lights in ever house went on

you could hear shotgun shells
being loaded from inside the carwinder
it was getting eat up good
tore out home
squalling like a banshee rooster
that other cat wasn't through
come after him

Vera's asleep
with her winder open
it was August
never heard a thing
she's too sick by then
that cat come in
went down under the covers
to go to bed and sleep with her
here come the othern
they had it out in the dark
between her legs

heard her in Tennessee
neighbors come running
thought it was a tragedy
her being raped or dying
they wanted to see
Boyd Carr come through the backdoor
run in her room
turnt on the light

she's standing on her bed
with her nightgown pulled up
over her head
he sed her belly had blood
and slobber and catsnot
all over it
that cancer poked out
like she's pregnant on one side

or a watermelon grown there
her stomach looked like
whatall was in there
had a pocketknife
trying to cut its way out
she couldn't stop
hollered with her mouth
wide open as her eyes
Boyd sed it scairt him so bad
he only seen that bump on her belly
and her face
he thought the devil got her
he wanted out of there
left without turning off the light
Ellis Britton sed by god
he'd of made sure he seen
more'n that
it was principle

they called Doc Kitchens
cause it was so late
he's only one come out at night
he's drunk
sed she'd be okay soon's she sober up
taken and given her a shot
they sed Doc she don't drink
she's got the cancer
he sed it's bad I seen worst
but that's gone taste when she chews it
shot put her back to sleep
but the cat was arredy gone
we didn't see it no more

she died anyway
in the hospital a coupla months later
they just opened the doors

after her funeral
let all them cats out
then closed them up so they'd run off
and got a new County Treasurer
wouldn't nobody take one back then
we didn't want the disease

Broken Leg

John I sed how'd you do that?
It's none of your dam business
if I fell off a loading chute
and busted the little bone 2 inches
from my ankle or I'd be crippled forever
instead of just in a cast
5 goddam weeks with 3d crop
needing to be cut

you're posta ast if its anything
you can do to hep out
not stand there looking to see
if its any blood showing
go get on that swoker for me
and cut Met Johnson's hay
before he passes a conniption
and has a spasm

it ain't that bad anyways
back home this Landrum boy
didn't have no luck with his leg
run over it planting corn
with a tractor 9 years old
when he clumb off to see
if the seeds was stringing out right
in 3 places they sed
and put a pin still there in it
he busted it or the othern
twicet more in the school
on football and baseball
one year and the next

before he got in a car wreck
with his daddy's pickup

calt his mama that night
law sez your boy he's done hurt hisself
she sed is he dead?
law sez no but it cut his foot off almost
a big piece off the side and toes
she sed is it something he
can bring home in a jar of pickled alcohol
from the hospital?
law sez no I don't think so

I think it's somewhars in that wreck
we had to prize him loost
that part stayed in
she sed well thank the Lard for that
can he get home by hisself
or do I have to come get him
and start the car
this late at night?

he's in a leg cast up to his knee
for months on crutches
so when it got bored
he's shooting a waspnest with coaloil
up in the shed eaves
in a watergun
here they come
he forgot about that leg and foot
took off running
got halfway crost the yard
before his leg remembered
the crutches by the shed door
it all give out

his mama heard the kitchen screendoor
turnt and he crawlt in
with a spraint ankle on the good leg
and his knee out of socket on the othern dangling
wasp bites all over his face
and one up his nose swolt up
like a pineapple
she sed if it's not one goddam thing
it's a dozen
is it anything else busted?
he said no ma'am I don't think so
can you get to a chair by yourself
she sed but not in here
I'm snapping beans for supper
go in the living room or somewhere
you don't turn my stomach
so he did

he didn't bust no more
of his bones after that
for a longtime
he got the faith and learnt his lesson

so before you go cut that hay
would you look round
brang me a fly swatter or clothes hanger
unscrewed so I can get it down
in my cast
this sonofabitch has got a place
if I don't itch it I'll die
I caint get to it
I left the keys to the swoker
on the kitchentable
you can find them if you'll look
on your way out
because I sure do appreciate

your offering to help out
the sick and afflicted
as your Christian duty

The Wart

*And when I passed by thee, and saw thee
polluted in thine own blood, I said unto
thee when thou wast in they blood, Live,...*
ЕZEKIEL 16:6

You ever had any warts?
I said yes, John, I have,
in high school and then two years ago
I had a bad one on my foot.
How'd you get them off
did you have to go to the doctor?
I said the one on my foot, yes,
he had to operate and said
it was the biggest one he'd seen.
How bout the othern?
John, I said, I cut one off
with a pocketknife and the other one
just went away.
By itself? he sed.
Sort of, I said and John sed
you found you a healer didn't you?

And I had to say yes because John was right
It aint never come back
has it? sed John and I said no
and it won't he said
this one I got's grown up right
between my fingers and it hurts
when I gript something
you think I can find me a healer
now when I need one?
I spoze I'll have to go to some doctor

and let him burnt it
but I'd as soon not

Mizrez Patrick back home
got one on her finger once
she couldn't have that she was rich
didn't want no scar where it was
so people could see she had warts
she went to old Mr. Cummings
the janitor in the grade school
for years till they had to finally retire him
then he was gateman
out to the cotton mill
everybody in town known him
wasn't nobody didn't like him
he raised us all
when we's in school
never forgot one of our names
when we got in the trouble
we'd have to go talk to Mr. Cummings
he'd make us feel so bad about it
wasn't no way we'd do that again
whatever it was
he could of cured Judast we all bet

so she went to him in the night
he taken them off
they's all gone in 2 weeks no matter
how many you had or where
she tried to offer him money
that's all she had by then
he wouldn't take it
never believed in it sez
it was a gift
it'd be ruint taking money
she sent him a card

she wrote herself and he kept it
I seen it when I's older

he was the best I known
for healing and could do it all
cured fire, thrash and warts
and could stop blood miles away
wasn't no doctor around
that could handle yellow thrash
they could do red and some black
they'd send them with yellow to somebody else
anybody to get them somewheres away
cause they didn't know what to do
but Mr. Cummings could suck it out
some of the doctors known it
would even send the kids to him

it was one baby had thrash so bad
his lips swolt almost shut
with yellow blisters and in its mouth
went down its tongue
in its throat before they brung it
he never sed a word
taken that baby
and held it down where he could
look in its mouth then
wadded up his hand in a roll
shaken that baby till it cried
its mouth come open
he put his hand over its mouth
and put his own
on the other side and sucked
he turned his head and spit
mebbe he sez some words then
I don't know
done that 3 times

give that baby back
to its mother and he sez
you clean that baby up
put some warshed clothes on it
you taken and warsh yourself
before you let that baby suck
if it don't get better in 3 days
you bring it back
if that thrash gets down
in its stomach it'll die
he never lost one
I bet he cured a hundred
I never seen him do it
I heard about it

and blood he could stop anywhere
he didn't have to be there
he known the Bible verse by heart
had it welded in
he could speak it
put in the name if he known it
in the right place
blood would dry up right then
over the telephone even

not just somebody
it was a horse run into a picketfence
rammed one up in his chest
when they pulled it out
blood came out like a waterhose
that horse was gone die
and it belonged to Wesley Stevens
broke out its pen and run off
trying to find something to eat
so it wouldn't starve to death
he fed them to his pigs

when they died that way
but he'd of said they stoled it
and killed it on purpose

it was worth 4 thousand dollars
a racehorse and sued them
they had to get that blood stopped
so they called Mr. Cummings
at the school sed please come down
he sed how far is it and where
tell me what that horse looks like
they did and sez you coming?
he sed no
that blood'll be stopping about now
it was just across the street
from where they's calling
they was mad and sez he's a liar
not to his face but when
they got back that blood
was down to almost nothing then stopped
horse lived
they had to pay for feeding him
while he healed up
it wasn't Wesley Stevens's fault

nosebleeds at school
cut fingers and bit tongues
school nurse would send them
right to him
he stopped a knife-cut in a fight
that man would of bled to death
doctor sed so
his vein was cut
doctor sed it wasn't no way
it should of stopped bleeding
but he didn't believe in it

he could throw fire out
him and his cousin Grace Nelson both
she's a womern and used her breath
he called it out and made it leave
Wart Thuett we called
this one I grown up with
real name Wallace Garland Thuett
when he's in grade school
they's taking the Saturday bath
it was cold
so after they got out the tub
in the kitchen they'd dry off
by the woodstove
it was Stewart Warner
he was little then
backed up to it to get warm
backed up too far
burnt a hole on his ast
against that stove
never had no clothes on

they called Mr. Cummings right then
on the telephone
sed that boy was burnt bad
where it might cripple his leg
he sed he'd be right over
he come and looked at that burn
arredy running together
he looked down in to it sed
I'm bringing that fire up
off the bone and out of his muscle
but I'm going to leave part of it on
he'll appreciate it
one day when he's older
they sed will he be cripple?

Mr. Cummings sed no
why'd you bring me here
if you wanted that?
he pulled that fire up out of him
using the Bible words and the faith
it took about a hour or 2
they sed you could see it boil out
and then here come a word
on that boy's butt they hadn't saw
it spelled *wart* right there
where he'd backed up on the nameplate
on the stove but that was all
that was spelt on him
Mr. Cummings left that
scarred on his ast
that's how he got his name
he never even missed
a day of school and set down even
he was healed
that was a hell of a lot better
name than Wallace Garland
you ask me

Worst was when the Baker boys
not Charley Baker's idiots
some different ones
got burnt in the lye pit
during pig-killing
and soap-making
had this big lye pit burning
kids playing pop the whip
so they could be in the way
while the people worked
Ralph Baker was on the end
of the line so they popped him
slung him off

he went right in that lye pit
lit on his back
burnt him from his heels
up the back his head
all his hair come off

his brother Dole
2 years oldern he was
walked in that pit
picked him up and carried him out
before the wormen seen
started hollering
they run him in the house
torn the rest his clothes off
put him on a bed
that boy was hurt
nobody thought he'd live
one sez call the doctor
anothern sez do that but call
Mr. Cummings and Grace Nelson 1st
then the doctor after
they can pull that fire out

Grace Nelson she come right then
but they couldn't find him nowhere
she went right to work
I seen every bit of it
put her hands over that burn
never touched it
they had to hold Ralph down by then
took 4 of them to keep him still
she moved her hands over him
away from her like she's pushing
the fire off from him
blown on it
with her head right down

over her hands
I don't know how she stood the smell
it was bad 3 times
and when she done it
whispered the words
at 1st we couldn't hear
but it took all night
after awhile she whispered louder
then talked trying so hard
some say we shouldn't of heard
or she could lose the power
you can only give it to one other
I don't know but what she sed was

> *There came a angel*
> *from the East*
> *bringing frost and fire.*
> *In frost*
>   *out fire.*
> *In the name of the Father*
> *the Son and the Holy Ghost*

that's what she sed over and over
I didn't hear nothing else
doctor come sed my godamitey
that's a bad one
we gone have to take him
up to the capital for a specialist
she sed not yet
I aint got it out or he'll die
and the doctor sed
yas I expect he will
that's too bad a burn
for him to live without a miracle
they worked on him
never give up

it was a hour or 2 later
bedroom door flung open
Mr. Cummings stood there
nobody ever got him
by the telephone we never known
how he found out about it
face all white
his eyes bugged out like a cow's
hollers get OUT of here
goddam you you aint welcome
popped our necks
we hadn't never heard him yell
or say such a thing
except his cousin
she never jumped or missed a breath
kept on whispering and healing

he talked to that fire
like it was a man cussing it
telling it to get the hell out of here
all night that room was crowded
with people trying to watch and help
nobody left and everybody sed
it was like they was a extra one
in that room you could count
I seen it too and I was only 12
back then in the corner
I never slept a minute that night
try to count the people
in there but it'd never come out the same
always one more
he called that fire every kind
of a sonofabitch
you can imagine all night
Grace Nelson kept on working
the wormen prayed

doctor did what he could
men stood back and watched
us kids set on the floor
by the wall till the sun came up

Mr. Cumming's face was as red
as hogblood
when he yelled Go
and don't never come back
he quit
him and his cousin had pulled
that fire out of that boy
doctor was as stupid as a duck
over it and couldn't believe it
they poured powder
for chapped ast from diaper rash on babies
to soak up the oil when it come up
that fire bubbled out of him
all night through that burnt skin
by morning they had it
up off his bone
where it would of killed him
it was only a burn
like you'd ironed him
with water blisters
that he could live over and not die
he did
not even scarred bad

they left him finally asleep
went in the other room
there was Dole who'd brung him
out of the fire
nobody'd remembered him
his feet was burnt black
Mr. Cummings sed oh no

why didn't somebody bring him in?
we never known they sed
is it too late?
he sed I don't know I hope not
him and Grace Nelson started over
but they couldn't get it all out
too much time had went by
it was in his bones

Dole's feet healed
but his toes wouldn't bend no more
when his feet grown after that
they grown right out
from under his toes
stuck up like peanuts
grown on top of his feet by summer
where he couldn't wear shoes
they finally had to cut them off
doctor sed he'd be a cripple for life
wouldn't never walk
except like a goose and limp
they took him to Mr. Cummings
he sed that's a lie
big toe was on both feet
he sed he'll walk just fine
if that's what he wants to do
it's up to him and his business
they sed would he pray over him
he sed what's the matter with you
don't you know how?
he sed they could do it
as good as him
they didn't need his help for that

it worked
both boys made it

Ralph had to make up his school
Dole walked just fine
but couldn't jump too good
Ralph couldn't neither
so we figured that was
his daddy's fault by birth
they both driving bread trucks
to grocery stores for different companies
somewhere in Texas

that night
might of saved my life
I's burnt in a oil well fire
where they thought I might die
spent almost 4 months
in the hospital
where they sed if I didn't die
I'd be scarred for life
burnt all over and the rest
of the crew that was burnt died
except one and he killed hisself
cause of the burnt scars
all over him where
you couldn't tell who he was
in the bed I remembered
what they done that night
to them boys
practiced it on myself
called that fire all I could remember
and sed her words
blown on it and pushed it away
I lived and don't have
no bad scars that show
but that was a long time after

so when I worked at the cotton mill

when I's older
one day I give Mr. Cummings
a ride home in my car after work
he seen my hand on the steering wheel
sed how come you got them warts
all over you
don't you want them off?
I sed yes but I didn't know how
he sed when you get home
they'll be tinkling a little bit
you take and put some castoroil on
then you forget about it

I'd forgot he could do that
last year R.B. McCravey
give me a nickel and bought
3 of my warts off the other hand
he done that for Homer McCreary
where he had one on his ast
where he couldn't set down
in a bathtub and he thrown
his nickel under the rug
they went away but I spent mine
so they come back
if somebody buys your warts
keep the money so they'll stay gone

they went away like he sed
in about 2 weeks I never noticed
then they was all gone
he'd just take thanks
no money
and they never come back
where they was then
but now this one
it's in a different place

right between my fingers
and he's dead
I don't know where to go
they aint no more like him
and it's a dam shame
you caint find a healer now
when we really need them

Idyll

You could find
Charley Baker's idiot girl
in the west pasture springtime
picking dandelions
grazing with the pigs
mind empty as sky

No bother
wind rooting her curls
she was happy in the flowers
waving half-acre handfuls
of gold coins
to the cars going by

Haystacking

GENESIS 3:17-19

Put them on the bottom row
side down so the wet
won't soak up so far
we'll square up from there
goddam I'm getting tired
I hope it's some supper ready
you ready for anothern?
I'll throw it right there
yougn snake it over
this is about the sorriest hay
I ever grown
but the price is so low
I caint afford to sell it

back home oncet
my brother he grabbed this bale
to stack it and seen it move
he thrown it down and looked
it was a rattlesnake got baled
in that hay trying
to get loose
he's working for that damned Bryant Williamson
who was so onrey
my brother oncet he borrowed
this other Mexican's hat with a high crown
like they wore when they come in
he put a roll of toilet paper
on his head and put that hat on
so when Bryant Williamson
chewed his ast up that day
my brother took off his hat

unrolled some paper
and wiped off the back of his head
Bryant Williamson sed good god
and that's all
never even offered to fire him
he's too mean to change by then
so my brother real careful
slud that bale on the stack
and left it with the snake in it
must not of worked
Bryant Williamson lived 10 more years
and he's arredy a old man
snake would of probley died
if it bit him

I'm working with Heavy one day
driving tractors springplowing
a section of land
both of us
and it took a long time
we'd plow up one side
then halfway back down
meeting going the other direction
we needed a drink of water
every time so we'd stop
and go to the well
under this boardarc tree
where it was a hose
one would pump and the othern
drink and take turns
this one time
it was Henry's turn to drink 1st
that was his real name
he picked up that hose
the end had mud plugged up
he taken and put his finger in unpushing

his eyes got big so he turned that hose up
looked
thrown it down
sez they's a snake in there
this little black racer
in there to keep cool
crawled out on the ground
that Eva McMahon had put in
back then when she's only 9
until she got back from school
and needed it
you'd of thought it was a alligator
the way Henry took off
we like to of died of thirst that day
it was only about a foot-
and-a-half long
but he never liked snakes
and got spooked

not as bad as that time
he's working at the car garage
they called him
over to Dr. Tubbs's office
to see what Wayne Runkles
brung in from the boyscout camp
where they's gone have Indin dancing
so these snakes
he's gone give some medicine
to make them drunk
do the dance with
and held some of them
in their mouths even like Indins
but this big one
they got out in the car
playing with it crawled off
through the heater

they couldn't find it no more
didn't tell him
just sed it was something underneath
he lifted that hood up
stuck his face down to see
it was a snake wrapped round
the fan pulleys sticking his black tongue out
at him about 9 inches away
he didn't know about and wasn't ready for
or he wouldn't of come anyway
hollered like a firetruck
slammed that hood on his hand
torn a fingernail off
run down the street hollering
4 blocks till he give out
he weighed 300 pounds by then
wouldn't come back to help
he sed they could haul that goddam car
to the dumpground
wouldn't even let Dr. Tubbs
fix his finger for free
he sed he'd find him anothern
to go to after that

Dan Cockrum and Hansford Hudman
put a bullsnake in a box
and when they seen Alberta Penny
coming down the street
give it to her
they told her it was some wine
but she couldn't drink it
on the premises right there
she taken it across the street
by the cotton gin
set down and opened it
hollered just oncet

for about 2 minutes long they sed
run away zigzagging
with her hands on her head
next day Dan Cockrum
tried to give her
a bottle of wine because she cleaned
his house on Thursdays
she wouldn't take it
sed you about given me a spasm
I don't want nothing from you
I'll get it myself
she stole 2 bottles
of his good whiskey
when she come to work next time
never touched the cheap bottle oncet

that summer
they had a grass fire
he was a volunteer fireman
helped put it out
and this night looking
for fires where it had arredy burnt
to water if the wind changed
he was walking in front of the firetruck
without his shoes on
cause he had a blister and the fire
burnt up the stickers
like walking on carpet
till he stepped on this soft cowturd
he known it was a snake
jumped straight up
before he come down
truck drove under him
lit on the hood and mashed it in
they took the money out of his check
to fix it because it was his fault

it wasn't no snake there
only cowshit he stepped in
fire department wasn't responsible

George Bird stepped on one oncet
walking along barefooted
known exactly what it was
when his foot went down
stood there like Moses' statue
never even finished the verse
of bringing in the sheaves he's singing
that snake commenced
to whipping its body around
them rattlers scratched up
the back of his legs
it went across them so many times
it was bruises high as his knee
he never looked down
to see his heel was
right on the snake's neck
just the head out under his foot
stood there with his mouth open
sed later he could hear
that snake snapping at him
his brother Edward seen it
run back to get the shotgun at home
George never moved one inch
till he got back almost a hour later
sez I'm counting 1, 2, 3
you can either jump
or I'll blow your foot off
sed tears come down his face
but he never bawled
counted and he jumped
that gun went click
he never loaded it

didn't make no different
he'd stood on it so long it was done dead
they figured thrashing round
it broke his own neck
and choked to death on it
Edward he put it on a canestalk
took it to the lefthanded ChurchofChrist
where his daddy was a preacher studying
but George Bird he wouldn't even go
sed he'd arredy had enuf snake for oncet
he'd wait and hear about it
in the sermon on Sunday

my brother thrown one at me
with a pitchfork doing hay
when I's on the wagon
and it hit me
I thought it was a kingsnake
but it was a rattler
that sonofabitch thought I'd duck
and let it go on over
till I heard it rattle
I jumped right on his head
it sprained his ankle I hit so hard
neither one of us would get on
that wagon neither
we unhooked the horse and rode home
without telling nobody
what was up there until they
unloaded it and then
we come back to work after that
it crawled off by itself

that's as high as I can throw
for now let's go in
have some supper and quit

I'm too hungry
and LaVerne sed she's fixing
a applepie to eat
mebbe that'll make it all worth it

so can you get that bale
squirmed up there and
finish off that corner like that yeah
for a haystack
of nogoddamgood hay
that's about perfect

Brothers

It was this boy named Phillip Chariot
his mama opened the Bible when he's borned
whatever she seen was it
they called him Bubber
he had this harelip that didn't show
inside his mouth
they all sed it must of went on up through
to the top because he wasn't very smart
it didn't matter
you couldn't understand him when he talked
it wasn't his fault
he mostly just set and nod

this other brother was real smart
went to school studying typewriter
had a good job downtown
whenever you'd ask or tell him something
he'd always say oh I know that
his name was Cephas Peter
they called him Junior or C.P.
it didn't matter
he'd say the same thing either way
he arredy knew it

Bubber one day he taken and bought this boar
at the auction
gave two dollars for it
it was old and not worth nothing
brung him home in the daylight
nobody paid no attention to Bubber
wallered that hog in the house

got him in the bathtub somehow
nobody seen it
got the gun down off the wall
killed that boar right there
and left him.

C.P. come home from working
went in to pee like he always did
hollers and comes out
Bubber's setting on the furniture
nobody else had saw it
he sez it's a dead hog in the bathtub
they all looked around
Bubber got up he walked to the screendoor
right before he went outside
before anybody could go see the dead hog
in the bathtub
he turned around
smiling they sed, big
you could see right up in that hole
in his mouth
clear as a new moon sed oh I knew that
they all heard him say it and then
he let the screendoor slam shut
when he walked out and left

The Landrum Geese

What time is it? Is it time yet for supper?
Go up to the house and tell LaVerne
to get some supper ready I'm hungry
no don't, goddam get back here right now
don't go messing with her about no supper
she's in her wrong moon turn this week
don't say nothing at all right now
she'll do it her way or not
you go and piss her off
it could mess up the rest of your life
and ruirn the whole evening
yours and my goose both would be cook

I known a man name Goose once
I grown up with Goose Landrum
that's what we called him
his daddy and granddaddy too
I never known that one
it wasn't their real names
they had Christian ones
his daddy was Harold
and I don't know his granddaddy's
but it was something
Leon or Albert like that I imagine
his was George
we never called that to him
where'd I put them longhandle pliers?

it started with his granddaddy
which had his wife and this new baby

which later would of been his daddy
out to take a ride in the wagon
with this new team of horses
he was breaking in on a Sunday
so them horses spooked up a rabbit
scairt themselves to death and took off
like a slobbering whirlwind
he thrown her the reins
grapt that baby up and jumped off
tried to holler her to keep them
headed on the road best she could
till they given out
it was too late
sed her dress blown up in her face
she couldn't of heard him if she tried
screeching too loud by then
them horses sounded like a thunderbolt farting
she'd have to figure it out
without his help
she's a schoolteacher so he wasn't worried
it's her job to get paid to think of something
he had to carry that baby
all the way home walking
we didn't have no hitchhiking back then
most people had other things to do on Sundays

she got back that afternoon by about 4 o'clock
he was setting on the furniture rocking
when she come in the door
sed by god I'm hungry what we having for supper?
she sez whar's the baby?
he sed it's asleep in its bed
you sure are nasty you better take you
a bath after we eat something today
she never sed nothing

walked in that room to look at the baby he thought
started humming hisself a tune
got lost studying how it went
till he heard the cock
looked up and she had the rifle
pointed right at him out of the closet
he jumped and she shot
the middle rafter right out of that rocking chair
he run to the winder
tried to pull it up to jump out
it was froze he heard that gun go clock
ducked down on the floor
she shot the winder right on the cross bar
all four pieces of glass fell out
one of them didn't even break
anothern only busted in half
he crawled to the door till he heard it again
come up running hit that door
turned down the porch and saved his life
she shot that door through the heart and lungs
right where he would of been
if he'd of stood on the other side or went straight
he run as far as he could back behind the barn
where he could look through the board gaps
to see if she was coming after him
but she never
I think it's the bushing in the solenoid not rubbing
get me a screwdriver down here

he waited the rest of the day out there
by hisself to see if she'd leave
or burn the house down
nothing else happened
sed his dog wouldn't even come out
for company it was so ascaired too
stayed under the porch the whole time

he waited until after dark for something to happen
finally when it didn't
he snuck back up to see if she'd hung herself
or was hiding with that gun
got to the winder she was setting
in his chair staring at the bedroom door rocking
never even looked round sed
your supper's on the table if you want it
got up and went in and shut the door
he'd never made a sound so he never known
how she supposed he was there
that one friend of yours sez
all womern can see in the dark
I spoze they can hear through it too
it was catfish and mashed potatoes and fish gravy
with the head on looking at him
on that plate all in a bunch cold in grease
but he ate ever bit of it
he didn't think it was a good idea not to

she never offered to talk about it
and he had a story made up to splain
how she got free wagon-driving lessons
that could of costed upwards of 4 dollars
never got to use it
that baby was the only one
they ever had

from then on after that
you could walk up behind him
goose him or clap your hands
he'd turn inside out with a spasm
oncet these boys blown up
this blasting cap outside Josey's grocery store
he fainted right by the meat counter
talking to Jim Kennedy about bologna and Viennies

if he seen a gun he'd go white as a Yorkshire hog
you couldn't of offered to paid him enough
to come to town on the 4th of July
they'd of had to given him a transfusion
everbody called him Goosey
from then on

that baby grown up the same way
he was Little Goose in town
him and this womern had this baby
they name George which was my friend
before she run off to Oklahoma with a Indin well digger
his daddy was a Campbellite
didn't believe in no divorce or piano music
he waited for her to come back some day
but it was too late and she didn't
what they called him then was Poor Goose
he's ruint all over town
they'd all pray for him with the sick and afflicted
even the Lard known who Poor Goose was
but she was gone for good

before that
before they dug all them dry holes on their place
before Goosey the granddaddy hung and killed hisself
after his wife took off when Poor Goose grown up
even before he got behind on the taxes
and lost part of their farm and Kay Stokes picked it up
somebody give the grandboy they called Baby George
these 2 gooses for a birthday present
to be funny about it all
but he raised them for pets around the house
so one day eating supper they seen
them 2 going off down the road through the gate
Poor Goose sed there they go
you better get them back inside the fence

and close that gate if you want to keep them
that boy run out to do it

in a minute they looked out the winder
he had one goose under both his arms jumping up and down
they could hear him hollering through the wall
Leggo goose, leggo me goose
went out on the porch sed what's going on?
boy turnt round still jumping
both them long necked gooses had leant over
and bit him on the pecker
he squoze so hard one passed out
they thought it was dead
its head down flopping like a well-bucket
and they'd have to eat it but it wasn't
othern hung on until his daddy
jerked it loose but it was a tragedy
that goose flopped its wings and give him
a bloody nose
and it broke that boy's pecker
must of busted something in there
turnt off to the east
almost like the letter L ruirnt
took him both hands to pee from then on
he never did get married by choice
sed he never had no inclinations or otherwise
it was too much pain for being married to be worth it

so after that
after all the womern left and Goosey hung hisself
and Poor Goose and Goose Neck
which is what they called him at first cause it looked like one
was living alone out there together
for the rest of their lives
about to lose the rest of the farm during the drought
with no money coming in to nobody

before they noticed it them two geese
turned in to over a hundred
you couldn't come up to their gate even
here all them gooses would run up
with their wings and tongues out
hissing and squawking like a oil well fire
even the Jehovah Witnesses couldn't get up to their porch
they'd of busted your knees flopping their arms
then you'd slip on goose shit and fall down
they'd bite off all your private parts and ears
before you could crawl off and get away
and that saved the farm
is it a rag up there
I can wipe off this oil with?
no dammit not a clean one
one I can use on oil
you wearing a tee shirt?
take it off and give it here

M.L. Basinger come in
with the drilling and well supply
had his machinery and parts spread out
acrost his property
people started sneaking in and stealing it at night
dogs didn't help
they'd bring dead meat and feed them
walk around and take whatall they wanted
he's about to lose everything
when he heard about the Landrum geese
went out and offered them 5 dollars apiece
for as many as they'd sell him
made enough to pay the taxes
and keep the rest of the land
it stopped the stealing right now
bunch of field hands cut across Basinger's

one evening after work singing out loud
just got the gate close
there was all them geese
if they'd of kept singing it might of been all right
but they turnt round and went quiet
like something was the matter
that was what them gooses was looking for
it was like a bale of cotton busted in a hurricane
scairt them so bad they couldn't get that gate back open
tried to run but they couldn't get away
one fell down and about drowned hisself
on dry land holding his face in the dirt
so them geese wouldn't get his eyeballs and nose

tried to climb that fence with the barbwore on top
cut their hands up like it got caught in a gin grinder
tore their britches almost off going over
one got tangled up and his foot stuck
hung him head down on the fence
but them geese couldn't get to him on the other side
his face a inch away
this one goose trying to get its head through the fence
hissed till he had goose spit down the side his mouth
screamed so loud they thought it was a fire truck
all in the Spanish they couldn't understand a word of it
but them geese seemed to know what he wanted
made them so excited
you could hear it 4 miles away
had to cut him down with some pliers
they thought his ankle was busted
never found out
he hit on his head come up running
none of them field hands said they didn't never
see him again he was gone
them geese chased him down the fence

trying to get to him heading straight south
they had them some plans worked out for him
M.L. Basinger after that put up a sign
sed Keep Out this property is protected
by Landrum attack geese
you come through this gate you will probley die

it was such a good idear
everbody wanted to buy some of them geese
even Charley Baker for his junkyard
and tied that sonofabitch dog up with a chain
but somebody told them idiot kids of his
they could populate with a goose
so he had to let them go
but it was worth a try he said
that dog was too mean even for him
but it never bit them idiots even oncet

that's how the Landrums got by and
held on to their land selling geese
for all them years till they give it up
but now you know something most people don't
who lived here all their lives
they think them people was call Goose
because of what they raise
that's how come nobody can pass a history test no more
they don't know before from after
and most don't give a dam either way
just what's on television and have supper ready on time
which if you push too hard on when she aint in the mood
can get you in a lot of trouble
set the whole thing going all over again
like the way it works when you don't pay attention
sometimes your goose don't get cook
you have to live with it
and that can last a real long time

get in and turn the crunk over
let's see if this sonofabitch'll start yet
we'll drive to town and buy something to eat
if you need supper that bad before it's ready

Bobby Joe

if I should die before I wake…

I don't know if I believed in ghosts
before Bobby Joe Lee had his stroke

that big man we called Bull lying there
all them years in that hospital room

wasn't nothing they could do
but wait and see

if he'd try to wake up or let it go
he was like a lightning struck tree

didn't even know it was gone
alone in there, blind and lost

until the next firestorm come
to finish him off

Willie and the Water Pipe

Then you have done a braver thing
Than all the Worthies did
JOHN DONNE

Willie Dalton would of laughed
if he'd been there
for his own funeral
8 men carrying his box
any one could of
carried him off like a floursack
he never stood 5 foot tall
in cowboy boots or weight
a hundred pounds a day in his life
his own family sed they thought
that Dr must of throwed out
the baby and got the other part
to breathe he's so runty

he's a horse jockey
didn't have much choice of it
broke 3-year-olds ever spring
at all the ranches around
one time a man sed
in front of him it wasn't ever
no horse alive Willie Dalton
couldn't ride and he sed
that's a pile of crap
any horse could of throwed him off
on a day but he'd try
and get back on
it was some thrown him
right back off again on his ast
but he made good money at it

busted almost ever bone
in his body and his privates
one time or the other

it was a 4th of July picnic
we had for the whole town
back then ever year
had running and jumping
rassling in it
so Leon Bilberry this one year
whupped everbody that tried him
he sed it aint no man
in this town I cain't kick his ast
them words never even hit ground
before Willie Dalton was at him
jumped right up on his head
wrapped him up with his arms
one leg around his neck and the othern
under his armpit and elbow
hollering like a strangled bobcat
he'd pry something loose Willie
would grap him another way
couldn't shake him off
Leon sed it was like a octopus
had his testicles wrapped
round his head
finally he fell down
whichever way he rolt
Willie went the othern riding him
like he's breaking a mule
kicked his sides so hard he thought
9 ribs was busted
it was only 2
till he give up Willie sed
say calf rope he did
say I give he did

say I won't never rassle Willie Dalton
never again he did
on his mother's white butt her watching
anything to get him off of him
he wouldn't rassle nobody after that

but what Willie done
that nobody else in our town
ever done before or since
was clean out the water pipe

town water come from
the mountain 7 miles
for ditch water and 4 drinking
so one spring both pipes clogt up
they fixed the drinking by geography
went halfway down and cut
it wasn't no water
so half of that back up
till they found the plug 3rd cut
and got it out
but the ditch water was different
not plugged off just partly
couldn't get no full stream of pressure
they didn't know what to do
so at the town board meeting
Willie Dalton sed for 2 bottles of whiskey
I'll clean that pipe out
they shut off the water
from the dam and he clumb in
the next day crawled that pipe
7 miles down mountain
through a 16-inch hole by hisself
with a flashlight
breaking up the bumps
to the bottom with his body

all day
when they opened that headgate
it was 9 dumptruck loads of gravel
and rock come out of that pipe
he'd loosened up going through

he crawled that pipe
30 years ever spring
by hisself for 2 bottles of whiskey
even after he had a cancer
like half a cantaloupe
hanging off his neck
his whole skin yellow as squash
almost ready to die
that last time he didn't come out
till after dark
only 4 people left waiting to see
some of the rest sed
he's dead we'll warsh him out
in the morning sometime
give him his 2 bottles of whiskey
Roy Talbert sed you gone open them
we'll have a drink?
Willie sed bullshit
that's all

they was sitting on his mantle
the day he died a month later
not even opened
with a letter they read
sed if I'm dead you can open these
and all have a drink now on me
wasn't one man in town
even Curley Robinson who would
touch one of them bottles
I expect they still setting there

and the water pipe sealt itself up
2 years later with mud and rock
they never could clean out
all the farmers had to go to wells
because Willie wasn't there no more
they had to find another way
to get by without him

Postlude

I

It's at least two people who'll never forget
the day old man Cummings died
I heard he's about to give it up
so I went by to see whatall I could do
like everbody else who'd known him for all their lives
it was a whole roomful of people
already there first when I come
wasn't even no open furniture nowhere
so we stood up or set on the floor waiting
while the otherns rocked or clucked

then the Reverent Jackson shown up
Reverent William Robert Jackson Lard's servant
back when we's kids growing up
we never called him that
he went to preacher school and got his churchhouse
we didn't know him no more
him and his name both got put into the revised version
he stopped being one of us for then
come in that house and sed
Has Brother Cummings expired?
I didn't have no words to answer that
but Lucille Cummings who had been his in-law
back before his boy Eugene she married died in his pigpens
face down in the mud of a heart attackt
sed Nosir Reverent but it's close
he been in his coma for 3 days now trying
the Reverent sez Brethern
let us bow togethah for a word of prayah

held up his hand so the Lard would know to listen
never got to the end of the first line
telling god who it was talking
we heard old man Cummings
call through the door to him
sed Billy Bob would you come in here for a minute?
not very loud we barely heard it
just like we was still kids in the school
and Mizrez Pennington had took one of us
down to Mr. Cummings back then
for being a disruption of influence
sed Shut the door behind you please son
we never heard no more
it felt like a little wind
went through that house shivering
looking for a place to curl up and lain down
it was after that when I heard the bells

2

he wasn't in that room but a little bit
when the door come back open
you could see right then by looking
Billy Bob Jackson had been down to Mr. Cummings
he wasn't gone be no trouble no more
for at least a long time
some sworn his face shown like Moses
coming back from the mountain
but he could of been trying not to be crying
like people have to do when them things happen
he sed Mr. Cummings he's went on now

at first he wouldn't tell us no more
I don't think he ever did tell everthing
but he finally come round sez
He was whispering soft so I couldn't hardly hear

but I known he known what he was being told
we could see that because he quit talking preacher talk
we could understand ever word in his mouth
even when he finally sed that prayer for all of us
And then it was like he looked right past me
like it was otherns in that room besides me
he stopped whispering and looked where they were
then he sez Well hello
it's sure nice of you to come
I swear that room turned warm like summertime
you'd think you could smell clover hay in there
when I looked at him again he was smiling
I could tell he done gone and left

3

they all talked about it for days and years
we should of built him a statue
but those of us who'd of thought of it wasn't expensive people
so he's just buried instead
some sed it was his wife come for him that day
some sed his boy Eugene must of been there too
the elders and deacons sed it was Jesust for sure with angels
Billy Bob never sed nothing else about it
and neither did I
there wasn't nobody for me to tell
but when I close my eyes and think about it even now
I can hear that sound I heard back then
of some silver bells jinglejangling in the wind

Benediction

Ellis Britton was standing outside the churchhouse
after the closing prayer by hisself this oncet
you couldn't be there by him and say something
you never known what he would say out loud
he'd goddam this and ohjesustchrist anothern
everbody talking to each other listening
wondering why they didn't go ahead and kick him out
he never put no money in the collection plate anyway
but they known if they did
he'd burn the churchhouse down that night
and their house too if he thought they's in on it
this one time the Campbellites across the street
hadn't quite got done and come out to stare yet
was singing the closing song right before the prayer
come to the line
    will there be any stars in my crown?
Ellis he turnt round hollered loud as he could
through their front door open cause it was summer
    no not one
    not a fucking one
wasn't nothing nobody could do
but get in their car and drive off home
one man Lovard Peacock I think back then
about torn his 5 year old boy's shoulder out its socket
pulling him to the parking lot to get away
so nobody would think he sed it
when them Churchofchristers come out to see
only ones left was the Brittons and the preacher
cars pulling out of there like it was Indianapolis
Ellis Britton he grapt his wife by the arm
sed let's get the hell out of here

we don't have to put up with this one bit
that preacher was so embarrassed
he had to go across the street and apologize
to all them Campbellites standing there
so they wouldn't think he was responsible
for Ellis Britton saying such a terrible thing
even if it might of been true

so this one day I'm talking about
that preacher didn't want to be polite
he walked up to Ellis Britton over off by hisself
had to find the right thing to say so Ellis
wouldn't have something to thrown a fit about
the whole congregation standing there listening to see
sed Brother Britton your wife sure is looking nice today
Ellis Britton sed oh bullshit
she's so goddam fat won't none of her clothes
fit her no more
she gets up a sweat even thinking
about walking outside to get the mail
it soaks in to the furniture
where it smells like hogs been in heat wallering on it
you caint even stand to set there
it'll slime up your clothes so bad
your britches climb up in the crack of your ast
and stick the rest of the day
you have to peel it out at night
I believe she's the second fattest womern in the churchhouse
she caint find no clothes to buy in this town
even her underwears is too tight
the rubbers won't stretch enough
and it leaves a dent all night on her belly
they don't make them big enuf that we can find
so what I want to know Reverent
is whar does your wife go to buy her drawers?
by god if they can fit her

they ought to be able to have some for my Lorene
that preacher learnt his lesson that day
after that he let Ellis Britton stand by hisself studying
    sidewalks
outside the churchhouse when the services was over
just like everbody else had learned how to do before he
    come along

DAVID LEE was the subject of a recent PBS documentary, *The Pig Poet*. Winner of the 1995 Western States Book Award, Lee has also been the recipient of fellowships from the National Endowment for the Arts and the National Endowment for the Humanities. He lives in St. George, Utah.

BOOK DESIGN AND COMPOSITION by John D. Berry, using Aldus PageMaker 5.0 and a Macintosh IIVX. The text type is Adobe Caslon, designed by Carol Twombly in 1990, and the display type on the title page is Big Caslon, designed by Matthew Carter in 1994. Both are based directly on specimen sheets of William Caslon's original 18th century typefaces. Additional display type on the front cover is FF Kath Condensed Bold Inline, designed by Paul H. Neville in 1992. Printed by McNaughton & Gunn.